The Executed Vision Realizing God's Strategy for Your Life

Stacey Bawuuna

Publishing Service By: Pen Legacy®
Cover & Typesetting By: Junnita Jackson
Editing By: Candice Rigdon
Bible Versus Retrieved from You Version Holy Bible App, © 2008-2019, Life.Church

Library of Congress Cataloging – in- Publication Data has been applied for.

Paperback ISBN: 978-1-7364112-2-3

PRINTED IN THE UNITED STATES OF AMERICA.

Prelude

You have the vision…now it's time to execute it.

It's no mistake that you're reading this book at this very moment, at this specific time in your life. You have the thirst to upgrade every aspect your mind, body and spirit – all you need now is the blueprint to make it happen, and by executing the steps detailed between the pages of this book, the vision that you have for your life will manifest into your reality. Follow the blueprint, and watch your marriage, family, finances, career, health and spirit explode!

With every page you read, God will provide you with direction on how He will use your visions, gifts, and talents to provide you with blessings that you won't have room enough to receive. Your commitment to following these steps will usher you into prosperity, abundance, and more than enough overflowing health, finance and favor. It is my prayer that once you reach the final page, ministries will be birthed and flourish under your renewed passion to persevere. Read without doubt, knowing that God never fails.

I rebuke the spirit of fear, inadequacy, low self-esteem, laziness, procrastination and the lack of resilience inhibiting your ability to execute the vision for your life's purpose. I pray that you will allow your confidence in the Word of God to override anything and anyone attempting to convince you that you don't have what it takes to receive what's already ordained for you. If God called you to the vision, He's already provisioned it. You just need to define the vision, practice it, and take action.

Self-Declaration:

As of this moment, I denounce self-limiting thoughts and actions hindering me from living a life of abundance and happiness. I commit to dreaming bigger and aiming higher. I realize my full potential and will persist until I have fully executed the vision that God has given me for my life.

"But He continues to pour out more and more grace upon us. For it says, God resists you when you are proud but continually pours out grace when you are humble." James 4:6

Gracefully Broken

"When He breaks you, He doesn't destroy you, He does it with, grace." Tasha Cobbs,

Before I could become a loving wife, caring mother, author, lifestyle expert, podcast host and coach, I had to be broken. How else would I be able to speak life into others who are broken, unless I experienced the same breaking, beating and pressing? I was once broken, but when God put me back together, He positioned me to share the story of how HE gracefully reconstructed my life so that I could experience life more abundantly.

Coming from brokenness enabled God to position me where He genuinely wanted me to be. In every aspect of my life where God wanted more of me, He gently and carefully broke me - not to harm me, but to elevate me to receive all that He had for me. In the most intimate spaces of my life (marriage, motherhood, family, career), God removed the barriers keeping me from completely relying on Him. He no longer wanted to me rely on my ability, but cling to His power. God required me to exercise faith in trusting my husband, raising my children, and excelling in my career so that He could get the glory.

As you navigate through the steps of executing God's

vision for the sum of your life, allow Him to break the parts of you that need to be reconstructed. It won't be comfortable, but I am witnessing to you from a place of restoration, and I can tell you - it's so worth it! He will keep you through the breaking process. As you read each story of brokenness, restoration, clarity, breakthrough, and victory, remember that God is no respecter of persons; what He did for me and countless others, He will do the same for you, because you have the same grace to execute your vision.

Understanding Vision

"'For I know the plans I have for you,' declares the LORD, 'plans to prosper you and not to harm you, plans to give you hope and a future.'" Jeremiah 29:11

Goals and aspirations articulate our desires to do something important or extraordinary. The vision differs from a goal or aspiration; your life strategy is tied to creative power. That is, vision is the ability to imagine or plan the future with God's wisdom.

Your vision is a glimpse into your purpose. Some may recognize vision as a strong desire to conquer what seems impossible, while others may experience an inexplicable pull to achieve something out of the ordinary. Whatever the perspective, your vision is a calling to GREATER. Since your vision is adjoined to purpose, it isn't just for you, it's connected to someone's reason for living, trying, leaving, and believing. That means vision far exceeds goals, and as such requires a different approach to be carried out.

You were designed to impact lives, by living yours according to your purpose. It's important to know that everything that God has purposed for you is achievable, otherwise you wouldn't have the vision. So, if everything that God wants for you is achievable, why haven't you done it yet?

The answer is simple: There's a process for progressing from understanding to fulfilling God's vision for your life.

The first time I purchased a luxury car, I was excited just to get approved - especially considering my 580-credit score. It was hard work, but I improved my credit and established a decent savings to make my dream happen, and not-so-suddenly, I did it! Seeing the word APPROVED sent me to the moon and back. I couldn't wait to sign the contract and drive away in my dream car. I'd achieved what I wanted, and God blessed me to do it. But later I realized, I moved too quickly.

There were so many incentives that I could've gotten prior to signing the contract, but in my haste, I left the extras on the table. Keep in mind I got what I wanted - but not everything I was able to obtain. That's the difference between reaching your goals and executing your vision. God's word says that He wants more for us than we can ask for ourselves, which I failed to recognize. My oversight cost me the favor God tried to give me.

By the time I purchased my next car, I had a fresh perspective. I knew what I wanted, but also realized that in His infinite wisdom, God knew what was best for me. I repeatedly petitioned God to show me what He had for me and vowed not to move until I heard from Him, which took months of prayer. But I was faithful. And eventually, faithfulness paid off.

Suddenly, God provided the direction and clarity I needed to get my car. I didn't sit around all day, waiting for the best deal a salesperson offered; I had a vision, and I was in control. I didn't step foot into the dealership until it was time to pick up my vehicle, along with my incentives: key chain, iPad, hat, t-shirt, and two years of concierge service. All the perks, and a fantastic deal!

Do you see the difference?

Operating in vision and purpose opens the door to receive everything God has for you!

Take Action:

As you journey through this book, consider the following:

- What value does having a vision for my life create?
- What impact does lack of vision have on my life?
- What are the risks associated with lack of vision?
- How can I use the vision God's given me to create the life I'm truly supposed to live?

_____

_____

_____

_____

_____

_____

_____

_____

_____

_____

_____

_____

_____

_____

_____

First Seek God's Vision

"But seek ye first the kingdom of God, and His righteousness; and all these things shall be added unto you." Matthew 6:33

David Hudson said, "Do not have your concert first, and then tune your instrument afterwards."

Similarly, it's pivotal to understand that prioritizing God's vision for your life is crucial to gaining focus and clarity. We should **seek first** to understand God's purpose to experience all He has to offer. It's not to say that you can't experience success in your relationships, business and health, but God has so much more for you.

There are countless books and courses out there which teach about striving for and achieving your goals, and I've read many of them. Indeed, the authors of those books have attained certain levels of peace and success, but as I grew closer to God I wanted more. Not more success per se...I wanted more of God. I didn't want to simply achieve, I desired to glorify God and impact lives through alignment with His vision for me. While there's nothing wrong with setting goals, when you yearn to execute God's vision, you have to shift your approach. How do you shift? By first pursuing alignment with Him. Simply put: SEEK HIM.

You've likely heard the scripture, "Without vision, the people will perish." (Proverbs 29:18). Most often, this scripture is used as a starting point to set goals; however, let's explore it further.

Without God's vision, your achievements may not be in alignment with His plans for you. Think of it this way: If someone offered you $100.00 just because, you'd likely say thank you and take the money. What if you knew that the person offering you $100.00 had given another person $100,000,000 simply because they asked? You'd likely feel empowered to ask for more, knowing it's attainable.

I recently heard a story of a couple who created a vision board. On that board was a beautiful photo of a newly constructed home. Even though the couple desired the home they envisioned, first they wanted to align themselves with God's vision. They sought God daily, requesting clarity. Suddenly, God connected them with people and banks who could help manifest their dreams.

What the couple asked for and the detour God gave them far exceeded their expectations. So, when they encountered a roadblock with a realtor who insisted they get something less than what they wanted, because God had already shown them His plans for them, the realtor was dismissed, and they immediately connected with another one who not only secured what they asked for - it was at a lesser price!

That's how amazing God is. Seek Him first, and everything else will be added in abundance.

Take Action:

- Spend time with God, diligently seeking to understand His vision for your life.
- Set aside alone time with God each day. Ask Him for clarity on the vision He has for you.
- Listen to instrumental soaking music in gently guided worship. Pray with expectation for God to show you the vision. Write down what you see, hear and feel.
- Implement these steps as part of your daily routine. You'll be amazed to see what God reveals to you.

_____

_____

_____

_____

_____

_____

_____

_____

_____

_____

_____

_____

_____

_____

_____

_____

_____

_____

Envision the Life you Want

"Delight yourself in the Lord, and He will give you the desires of your heart." Psalm 37:4

Consider every aspect of your life. Relationships, career, mental, spiritual and physical health. What do you see, who are you with, what's your routine? All the components making up your ideal life aid in developing a plan of action to clarify your vision. Those strong desires that seem impossible. Those are your visions.

I have a sister in Christ who is one of the top strategists for a fortune 500 company. During one of our conversations when I called her completely on the edge, she asked me a question that totally shifted my perspective.

See, I'd just gotten promoted for the third time in less than two years, and my salary sailed well into six figures. I purchased a home in a prestigious neighborhood, and my marriage was the best it had ever been. Even with all those blessings, I wasn't fulfilled.

Though I was good at it, I didn't love the work I was doing. I was nervous about my doubled mortgage payment for a house needing tons of renovations. I secretly worried that my marriage would revert to the sunken place it was once in. Anxiety overtook my positivity, and I sank further and further into the pit, without seeing a way out. When I finally called my friend, I was broken and desperate for an escape from the fatal solutions to my problems plaguing my embattled mind.

Life no longer seemed to be worth living.

"What do you want most in life? "She interrupted my tears with such a simple, yet profound question.

Drying my eyes, I began to rattle off the things I had.

"Stop," she instructed. "What do YOU want? Think for a minute about what you would be doing if you didn't have to worry about anything. Where would you be, who would be surrounding you?"

Through our conversation, I began understanding that though it seemed like I had it all, God had more for me. His desire for us to fulfill our purpose is so strong, He'll cause us to be uncomfortable while caring for and elevating us. I was crushing my goals, but I wasn't in alignment with His vision. It makes me think of the difference between God's *perfect will* verses His *permissive will*.

God permitted me to achieve great things both professionally and personally, but that's what He allowed me to do. His desire for me was greater and more substantial than a nice house and a cushy job. I had to envision the life I desired to get closer to God's blessings tailored just for me. I began spending more time with Him, not only asking but *listening*.

The art to hearing God requires your undivided attention. I set aside 15 minutes each day to commune with Him; praying for five minutes and listening for ten. I wrote down everything I heard, saw and felt during that time. This method helped develop the complete vision, not just what I saw on the surface. It's amazing how 15 minutes a day made such a huge difference!

Take Action:

Envision your life without limits. Compile a list of questions like:

- What would I be doing if I didn't have to work for money?
- What am I doing when I'm most happy?
- What tasks do I complete effortlessly because they come naturally?
- When I think about my ideal day, month or year, who am I spending time with, where and why?

List all the aspects of the life you envision, removing limiting thoughts such as *that will never happen*, or *maybe if I were younger*. Write it all down, and if you find yourself hesitating about writing something, that's probably the very vision that God has for you.

_____

_____

_____

_____

_____

_____

_____

_____

_____

_____

Write the Vision

Habakkuk 2:2" The LORD gave me this answer: Write down clearly on tablets what I reveal to you, so that it can be read at a glance."

When I was a little girl, I had a *magic notepad*.

In my pad, I penned my desires and sure enough, after a while they'd come to pass. It was magic! Later in life, of course I realized that it wasn't the magic of the pad, but what I chose to focus on.

As the Global Talent Acquisition Leader for Operations for a major corporation, I traded my magic notebook for Microsoft products to construct goals and objectives. I developed strategies to acquire the right talent who aligned with the company's vision, which required developing and delivering that strategy, as well as assembling a team to execute it.

My first year in leadership taught me a hard lesson about the difference between goals and S.M.A.R.T. (Specific, Measurable, Attainable, Realistic and Tim based) goals. I spent much of that year responding to issues, reviving relationships and establishing reports to justify what was happening. Much of the hard work can be attributed to the fact that I hadn't determined why I made decisions which weren't connected to the end result. I needed to leverage S.M.A.R.T. goals to strengthen the strategy and prioritize the work.

The same holds true with documenting your vision. Blindly jotting down all the God's desires for you, leaves you without a starting point. Instead, you'll be sucked into whatever direction seems like the priority at the time. This is how most New Year's resolutions end up abandoned by February.

As I spent more time with God, I realized that when you ask, He delivers. The revelation came when I began feeling the way I did during my first year in leadership - all over the place. Wanting to write a book, start a podcast, appear on television...all simultaneously. The time I spent listening to God showed me that I needed to pause to organize all the invaluable information He was downloading.

When it comes to obtaining God's desires for you, it's like the company vision: broad and beautiful but requires work.

As you translate God's vision to goals, and goals to reality try using the B.O.L.D. (Big, Operational, Limited, Dated) declarations approach. Imagine a funnel with straight lines crossing from one end to the other, all the way down to the end.

B - The BIG vision.

O - Operational goals aligning to the vision.

L - Limited actions necessary to reach the goals.

D - Dated tasks necessary to complete each action.

Everything in the funnel is required for execution. Each component within the funnel is necessary and must connect to the item above it.

Start with:

(B) Big Vision: I would even say *audacious*. Vision is the corporate strategy for your life.

If you can accomplish your goal on your own, then it's just that, a goal. But a goal that supersedes your abilities, resources, knowledge, and requires faith - that's a big vision. Big vision requires you to rely on God by exercising your faith. God's vision is greater, broader and goes deeper than ours. If He gives you a vision for your life, and your reaction is, *How's that even possible?*, chances are you've received a big vision. (i.e., write a bestselling book that will be translated into 25 languages and transform lives across the world).

(O) Operational Goals: The steps necessary for activating the vision. This step breaks the large vision into smaller steps. Operational goals should be realistic. For example, writing a 200-page book in less than a month without a topic or a computer might be unrealistic. In this case, your operational goals would be: Choose a topic for book, Create an Outline, Research Similar books, Create a Draft, Find a Publisher, etc. until the publishing process is complete.

(L) Limited Actions: God's broad vision doesn't mean you need to execute all of the steps at once. You need to prioritize. Part of prioritization is filtering menial tasks from necessary ones to gain clarity and focus. (i.e., purchase a computer for writing, set aside time to write, finish the book, and embark on world tour).

(D) Dated Tasks: Action requires deadlines, otherwise they can go on forever. Setting deadlines for tasks helps hold you accountable to yourself. (i.e., purchase computer on January 3, 2021, set aside two hours each day to write five-ten pages per week, complete 200-page book by DATE).

Take Action:
- While planning is essential, you can spend too much time doing it. ACTION propels the vision. Document the actions you need to take, then execute them.
- What steps do you need to take first, second etc. to make your vision come to life?
- Use your Notebook to translate 3-5 goals into BOLD declarations.

_____

_____

_____

_____

_____

_____

_____

_____

_____

_____

_____

_____

_____

_____

_____

Keeping the Vision in Front of You

"The LORD said to Abram, Look as far as you can see in every direction—north and south, east and west. I am giving all this land, as far as you can see, to you and your descendants as a permanent possession. "Genesis 13-15

Once you've written your vision, it's imperative to implement it as part of your daily routine to manifest it to reality.

The reason this is such a vital part of the process is because what you meditate on gets into your spirit. You see, God already planted the seed, but you have to nurture it to reap the harvest! What a man thinks is what he is; if you don't keep your vision in front of you, negativity (such as unforgiveness and condemnation), clutter your mind and steal your focus. Focus on God's vision, by mediating on it. Constantly keep it in front of you - read, write, execute. Chances are, if you're at least 30 and I ask you to multiply 6X8, without a second guess you'll answer 48.

On the other hand, if I ask you to name the capital of Istanbul, you may hesitate.

Why is that?

In school, teachers drill multiplication tables in your head, knowing it's the basis for all math. Now you may have learned the capital of Istanbul in geography, but you may not remember it so quickly when asked. While you studied both math and geography in school (probably acing both subjects), math required constant practice. You could argue you've had to meditate on math to keep it at the forefront of your mind, which makes sense. Just like math, you have to keep God's vision at the forefront.

Review the vision repeatedly, so nothing less important blurs your focus. When I was in school, the walls of the classroom were lined with multiplication tables. The tables were also printed on the back of my notebook, not to mention there were laminated copies on the desks. The tables were consistent reminders how prominently math would fit into my life. That's why we should keep our vision where we can see it; to remind us how important it is.

I remember when a friend of mine wanted to purchase a home, with a poor credit score and no sight of where the down payment would come from. However, she couldn't shake the feeling that God wanted her to purchase a home. It seemed impossible, yet she professed to close friends that this was the year that she was going to buy the house. Every time we talked, she boldly reiterated that her house was on its way.

I purchased a key chain for her that said "HOME," because I believed in her vision. My friend connected that chain to her car keys and carried it around without fail. Every time she started her car, HOME stared back at her. After a while, she purchased items for her home, storing them in places where she'd see them every day. Whenever she glanced inside the kitchen or walked past something she hung in the hallway, she declared, "Thank you for my house, God."

What she did was exercise her faith, keeping God's promises at the forefront. Then, she took *action*. She enrolled in a program for first time home buyers and put in the work to make the vision manifest; every aspect of the process seemed to be moving with ease. By the time she discovered the house she wanted to purchase, the realtor told her that not only would was she approved, but her interest rate was the lowest she'd ever seen in all her years of selling homes. God gave her more than she even imagined because she kept the vision in front of her and exercised her faith.

If God can give her what she asked for, He'll do the same for YOU.

Take Action:
- Declare that you have what you envision. The power of life and death is in your tongue. Speak about your vision as if it's already yours.
- Keep the vision in front of you to remind you of what God has promised. Many companies keep their vision and mission statements visible on walls, desktops, or intranet home pages. It's important to display them where they can be seen, because strategy drives the company vision. The same is true for your life strategy. Keep your vision at the forefront to remain focused on what you're working towards. Create a vision board from pictures aligning with what you want to accomplish or create a board on Pinterest.
- Prepare to meet your goals, revisit the actions required to achieve them, then implement them into your daily

routine.

- Display reminders of your vision somewhere they can be easily viewed every day.

_____

_____

_____

_____

_____

_____

_____

_____

_____

_____

_____

_____

_____

_____

_____

_____

_____

_____

_____

_____

_____

_____

_____

_____

Divine Connections

"As iron sharpens iron, so a friend sharpens a friend." ~ Proverbs 27:17

You probably have it already.

Executing your vision isn't a solo act. You need to connect to people for a specific purpose. Depending on your vision, you may need a professional network, or a spiritual network if you desire a closer connection with God. If your vision centers on familial changes, you need a village. Collectively, this makes up your divine connections.

Divine connections are a collection of individuals or entities consisting of family, community, professional, and spiritual relationships essential to executing a vision. Some of these connections may be chance meetings that inexplicably advance at an accelerated pace; others may be steady, consistent connections spanning across more than a single entity.

After identifying the steps needed to take to shift your dreams to reality, think about who can assist you along the way. Your divine connections are vitally important to executing your vision, as they serve different purposes.

For instance, a few years ago, I attended a six-month leadership course where part of the curriculum focused on the art of network building. Although it was a professional development course, one of the discussions explored the cross sections of relationships. Some relationships begin professionally then evolve into friendships, while others start off as mentor-mentee, transforming into peer mentors over time.

What struck me the most about what I learned was that regardless of the relationship, at the core of them was a connection, no matter how brief or long. Up until that point, I hadn't been very intentional about building my network; I had mentors, mentees, peer advisors, and advocates, not to mention pastors, prayer partners, and my beloved village where I've held relationships spanning from less than a month to 35 years. What I learned through that course; however, is that to develop, you need relationships that will position you to dream big, aim high and finish strong.

Where God was taking me required me to be intentional about who I connected with. Not for what they could do for me, but how we could grow each other. Within my divine connections, are visionaries, business leaders, executives, ministers, educators, attorneys, prophetess, authors, coaches…the list goes on. The point is, is that within my network there are people headed where I've been, and others who've been where I'm going. I can pour into someone and have someone pour into me. Divine connections are built on trust, which is necessary for associates to challenge, disagree with and push you towards greater. When you have a vision for your life, you have to leverage your divine connections to propel you forward. You can't do it alone.

Take Action:

Think about the three areas of divine connections:

- Who do you have to push and challenge you?
- Who's where you're trying to get to?
- Who can get into rooms that you don't have access to yet?
- Who needs to hear your story?

Write a list of connections from each of your networks - spiritual, professional and village. If there are areas where you are disconnected, seek God to add to that area, then reach out to people. Pick up the phone, contact through LinkedIn; don't be afraid to start the conversation.

_____
_____
_____
_____
_____
_____
_____
_____
_____
_____
_____
_____
_____
_____
_____
_____

Prepare for Distractions

"Overhearing but ignoring what they said, Jesus said to the ruler of the synagogue, Do not be seized with alarm and struck with fear; only keep on believing." Mark 5:36

God has given you talents to use for His purpose.

You've felt the desire to do something spectacular, but you keep waiting for yet another confirmation. You've allowed fear of failure to prohibit you from carrying out God's will for your life and limited your abilities and resources as an excuse to abort the mission.

If God has given you the vision, He's already made provisions. Despite what it looks like in the natural, God's already paved the way - you just need to move forward and carry out the plan. Stop worrying about how you're going to make it happen because YOU can't. Though you can't see it, God's already made it happen - your job is to carry out the orders that you've been given. So, stop planning and start DOING. Open your restaurant, go back to school, accept the promotion, ask for the raise, start the ministry, ask her to marry you, buy the house. Don't worry that the bank may not approve you, the school's too expensive, someone's more qualified or that you haven't run a ministry before…just do what you know God has called you to do.

Stay focused!

Have you ever seen a presidential motorcade? It moves at a steady pace. The drivers are instructed not to go above or below a certain speed and don't be concerned with what's in front or behind them because the police and secret service clear traffic, protecting them at all costs.

Now the driver usually can't see who's working on his/her behalf, but just like clockwork by the time they reach an intersection or crossroad, it's cleared. It's imperative to their safety (and the president's) that they follow instructions to keep from getting sidetracked…or ambushed. Someone could be injured or killed.

Our lives are like the president's motorcade. We've been provided with instructions and protection for our destiny; by staying the course and traveling the speed that's been designated for our assignment, we'll reach our destiny safely. Too often, we're distracted by what's in front (future worries), behind (past hurts) or on the sides of us (stuff that has nothing to do with us), slowing down or stopping all together to deal with those distractions.

Stop!!!

It's delaying your destiny and just like that motorcade, slowing down or delaying the process impacts the others in your caravan (your family, prayer partner, admirers who you aren't even aware look to you for inspiration). Don't get caught up in the distractions, because you're covered. The mess that seems to be ahead of you is merely another distraction; don't stop, don't hesitate, or detour. Just GO. Remember - what you may not see is that the road's already been cleared.

Distractions deflect from what's important. They breed

confusion, and disorientation. Executing God's vision means inevitably encountering distractions; since you know that you have the upper hand, get prepared.

The enemy's vision is to steal, kill and destroy. He wants to steal the vision by shifting focus away from the vision to the distraction. My pastor teaches that anything contrasting with what God says is a LIE. Learn to spot the lie and you can overcome the distraction. How do you spot the lie? By meditating on what God says about you and arming yourself with His promise so that wherever anything in your life contradicts with what He says, you still WIN.

For example, God says:

- **Prepare for Distractions**. What distracts you? For some people it's alcohol, television, or procrastination. Ask God to reveal what your distractions are, write them down, then learn to identify the signs. Worry, confusion, and agitation, are a few signs of distraction. In your research, you may find you worry about situations God has already worked out. Or maybe there's ambiguity in the actions you're taking, or something feels off. Those closest to you are often used to distract you, your children are agitating you, or a friend is testing your patience. Recognize the distraction for what it is, then strategize.
- **Meditate on God's Word**. Develop a counter strategy. If you know that you have something to do towards your vision but indulge cocktails at the end of the day before you've put in the work, you're already distracted. Instead of procrastinating, commit to removing the distraction completely or until you've

completed your task. This is a good time to fast from indulging in what distracts you and make a habit of spending time with God to give you strength to remain focused.

- **Exercise your authority**. Knowing what God says helps you stand firm and repeat it to the enemy when he tries to distract you.
- **Find peace in the distraction**. Getting distracted indicates that you're on the right track. Realizing your purpose through the execution of your vision isn't easy work. It takes commitment and focus. There will always be distractions to face, and the closer you get to reaching your goals, the more distractions will come. Celebrate! You're getting closer, you're almost there. Don't let the distraction win, because you already have the victory.

Take Action:

Write down your distractions and how you plan to counteract each one. Having an accountability partner helps spot and counter your distractions quickly. Celebrate when you spot a distraction, (1) because you recognized it and can take action to overcome it, (2) you're just that much closer to realizing the life you envisioned.

Even if you're unable to prepare for a specific distraction, you can still implement your strategy once you recognize it. The day I sat down and committed to completing this book, I found a lump in my armpit. As a woman in her forties, this caused concern. My initial reaction was to panic, but quickly I recognized it as a distraction. God had already given me the vision to finish this book, so regardless of the lump, I refused to let it stop me. So, what did I do? I strategically conquered the distraction by immediately reciting a prayer of thanksgiving and expectation.

I told God that I was expecting to fulfill His vision for this book, and for my life. I reminded the enemy what God says about me, because he already knew: I am healed, and my days will be long on earth. I cast down every imagination not in alignment with what God has for me, and spoke to the lump, telling it that it had no place in my body. After completing these steps, I scheduled an appointment with my doctor and continued writing.

The important takeaway about distractions is that distractions will come, but it's how you prepare for and respond to them which make a difference in moving forward. Don't stay there in the midst of the distraction - move forward with the vision.

_____
_____
_____
_____
_____
_____
_____
_____
_____
_____
_____
_____

Acknowledge Your Past and Move Forward

"Forget the former things; do not dwell on the past. See, I am doing a new thing!"
Isaiah 43: 18-19

Every one of your experiences was necessary for you to grow, build character, and carry out your vision with purpose. Every setback, loss, relationship, opportunity and victory has prepared you for this moment. Accepting and dealing with your past permits you to rebuke the spirit of condemnation and prohibit the past from dictating your future. Embrace the lessons, but don't allow them to own your emotions. Operate from a place of wisdom moving forward.

We know from the last chapter that distractions can manifest in the form of past hurts and guilt, so for you to move forward with God's vision, you need to separate your old self from the new you. I want you to say this out loud:

I am not my past!

Now say it again.

Okay, scream if you need to...just believe you truly aren't your past.

2 Corinthians 5:17 - *"Therefore, if anyone is in Christ, he is a new creation. The old has passed away, behold the new one has come."*

You're not the same person you once were, so don't let anyone - especially yourself, get in the way of moving forward in receiving all that God has for you, simply because of past mistakes. Skipping this step paves the way for discouragement to deter you from executing your God-given assignment. Let the past remain where it is - the new you doesn't have room for doubt and condemnation; God's already delivered you from that. Out of every situation you've encountered – whether God's will or not, you're still here…forgiven and renewed. Walk in your newness, without permitting the past to corrupt the vision for your future.

May I share this? A friend of mine was unfaithful in her marriage. She struggled with infidelity, but after much hard work, prayer, and therapy she and her husband reconciled. Soon after, God blessed her with the vision to teach a course on marriage and healing. Immediately, the thought of going public and being transparent about her infidelity nearly sank her vision prior to executing it.

What happened?

My friend allowed the old actions she'd been delivered from to resurface and convince her she couldn't do what God already ordained she could. Because she recognized this as a distraction, she executed her distraction strategy, which included:

- Declaring she's no longer the OLD person.
- Recognizing there are people who might not accept it, but she's approved by God, and that's what matters.

- Identifying scriptures and affirmations speaking to who God says she is.
- Creating reminders that she's ordained to share what God's given her to create.
- Committing to letting no distraction, past boyfriend, or scorned associate condemn and distract her from executing God's vision.
- Posturing herself to receive every good thing God has for her, leaving nothing on the table.

As a result of acknowledging her past and handing God the broken fragments of her life, God restored my friend's marriage and moved her to a new location. She purchased a house, birthed a ministry, wrote a book and taught others to how to heal their marriage. Most importantly, not only did God forgive her, but He anointed her husband to gracefully forgive, moving forward in truth and honesty. Her husband later said to me, "Our marriage is the best it's ever been, because we learned how to rely on God to guide us by showing us the true meaning of His love."

Take Action:
- ✓ Document past hurts and guilt you're carrying. This takes some time but commit to it. It's necessary to move forward.
- ✓ Acknowledge what you've done and what's been done to you.
- ✓ Declare you are forgiven and forgive those who hurt you.
- ✓ Accept that as a new person, you no longer carry the weight of the old you. Because if you don't, you can't carry the blessings in store for you.

- ✓ Find scriptures or affirmations which speak to who you are.
- ✓ Make it a practice to acknowledge that you are not your past, any time it attempts to block your vision.
- ✓ Position yourself to receive all God has for you. Leave nothing on the table.

_____
_____
_____
_____
_____
_____
_____
_____
_____
_____
_____
_____
_____
_____
_____
_____
_____
_____
_____
_____
_____

Unforgiveness

"Love prospers when a fault is forgiven, but dwelling on it separates close friends."

Unforgiveness is a vision killer. If you have someone you need to forgive, someone you need to request forgiveness from, or if you need to forgive yourself, do it.

Remember the opening chapter on being gracefully broken? Forgiveness falls into this category. God wants to remove the barriers prohibiting you from executing your vision. He doesn't want anything prohibiting you from doing what He asks of you. For example, if God gives you the vision to quit your job and travel the world to speak on relationships, but you are harboring unforgiveness towards your ex-husband and his new wife, you're not going to truly fulfill God's will until you forgive. God wants to fill you with all of Him, but you limit Him when you refuse to forgive.

There were times when I needed to be forgiven by others, times that I needed to forgive, and there's also been times when I've had to forgive myself. In relationships of any kind, if forgiveness is needed it must've been preceded by an act of intentional or unintentional hurt perceived by the person asking for it.

Most people don't set out to hurt the ones we love, but in many cases the most devastating hurt we experience comes from those we love the most, mostly because we expect more from them. Our expectation of how we should be treated, valued and loved may not perfectly align with the way someone else sees it. I wonder how often you've experienced or witnessed conversations between loved ones stemming from misplaced expectations which lead to disappointment and require more work to forgive.

Many years ago, I had to forgive someone who hurt me immensely. It was the kind of hurt you believe you'll never recover from. I went through of the motions of forgiveness, praying for a forgiving heart, verbally declaring forgiveness, and tried to move on. On the surface, I forgave them. Several years later, when I asked God to show me the areas of my life that were broken…He showed me this relationship.

Even in the middle of praying, I paused with the thought I'd already done what I needed to do to forgive, shrugged it off and continued praying with the assumption that the conviction I felt was a miscommunication between me and God. But you know, just as I do, God doesn't miscommunicate, but we certainly misinterpret.

Later that week, I was presented with a speaking opportunity, and when I read the topic, I was thrust back to that hurtful moment in my life. Before I realized it, I was sobbing inconsolably in my kitchen while gripping the invitation in my trembling hands. If you know me, crying is not my norm.

"What's happening?" I wailed into the air.

A quiet voice replied, "I'm showing you the areas of brokenness that need to be healed through forgiveness."

See, when you're the one required to forgive someone, it isn't a simple exchange of words, it's a process. There's the act of forgiveness taking place, but it needs to be followed by healing. The same process is true of being forgiven.

I've heard the process of being forgiven described as repeatedly being prosecuted for a crime, wading through judgement followed by conviction, then sentenced despite already being tried.

This is the intersection between the extender and recipient of forgiveness. The forgiver can forgive, but the healing process will take them through a series of sometimes unpredictable stages leaving the one being forgiven on edge, constantly feeling judged and sometimes living in fear. Often in relationships, forgiveness is preceded by prior events leading to offense. Once I realized I hadn't totally forgiven, I asked God to show me how to truly forgive and completely heal. To do that, I had to revisit the beginning and determine the events leading up to the offense requiring forgiveness, followed by:

- ✓ Admitting I was still hurting.
- ✓ Examining aspects of my life impacted by the offense.
- ✓ Accepting that erasing the past isn't an option.
- ✓ Exploring areas where I may have contributed to the conflict.
- ✓ Empathizing by separating the act from the person.
- ✓ Actively working on healing myself.
- ✓ Truly forgiving.

Once I vetted the process of truly healing, I felt peace. I remember feeling physically lighter once the burden of unforgiveness lifted. That's because on the other side of forgiveness is healing, love, prosperity, and if you want to remove those things blocking you from getting all God has instore for you, forgiveness is necessary.

Take Action:

✓ Ask God to reveal the areas of your life where you may need to forgive or be forgiven. Then write down the forgiveness steps and implement them in your routine.

_____

_____

_____

_____

_____

_____

_____

_____

_____

_____

_____

_____

_____

_____

_____

_____

_____

Remove Fear

"For God has not given us a spirit of fear, but of power and of love and of a sound mind." ~ 2 Timothy 1:7

Fear of failure is the biggest vision killer.

Many people never even start executing their vision because they've already anticipated failure as an outcome. While failure is sometimes probable along the journey, it's not a final destination; it's a temporary stop.

One trait successful people have in common is their refusal to accept failure as their final destination. Countless memoirs and biographies document the times when highly successful people "failed" along their journey. What's important; however, isn't the failure itself, but the lesson in it. Because after the failure comes the WIN.

Sometimes the lesson is to plan better, or to pay closer attention. Other times, the lesson is to keep going, strive harder, and don't quit. Each of us has a journey that will be filled with success and failure; it's important not to let failure block us from reaching our goals. If the first book flops, write another. If the business plan fails, find the gaps and keep moving. If the treatment didn't work, don't lose hope.

Failure is not your destination.

To get over my fear of speaking, first I had to figure out why I was afraid. By identifying what it was making me nervous, I realized I was afraid of not getting things right. What if I messed up? As I dug deeper, it became apparent that it wasn't the fear of getting something wrong per se, but it was the fear of not having my thoughts or ideas accepted. I was scared senseless of rejection.

Identifying the root cause was just the beginning.

Next, I read books on denouncing negative opinions of others, as well as scriptures and inspirational books about tapping into God's power inside of me. What really helped calm my fears was when I began operating according to my vision. Once I aligned my vision to God's purpose and sprang into action, I was empowered to walk into any room filled with people to speak on a subject where I wasn't considered an expert. And I did it well, knowing God equipped and positioned me to do it.

There's a certain confidence and authority we assume when operating according to God's vision for our lives. For instance, one of my children came to me in a panic, tears streaming, huffing and puffing and I thought for sure he was hurt. When I asked what was wrong, he said that his siblings had taken his toy and wouldn't give it back, even though he asked them to.

"Tell them to give it back," I instructed him.

"I already tried, Mom. They won't listen." He choked back the tears watering his eyes.

Incredulous, I said, "Tell them I said to give it back…now."

His entire demeanor changed after that. He stood up straight, wiped his eyes and the cutest smirk stretched across his face. He raced back to his siblings and with a loud clear voice he commanded, "Mommy said give me the toy back, right now!"

What happened?

My son knew he had the authority not to ask, but to demand his toy back. Because of the authority he'd been given, he went back with confidence, expecting to get what he asked for. If my son can operate on my authority with such confidence, then how could I not enter a room with confidence when the Almighty Himself told me to go?

Take Action:

✓ Identify 3-5 fears you have that are impeding your ability function as needed.

✓ Evaluating each fear, identify their source.

✓ Once you determine the origin, begin counteracting fear via scripture, therapy, etc.

✓ Face your fears head-on, so you can overcome it and operate in your authority.

_____

_____

_____

_____

_____

_____

_____

_____

_____

_____

_____

Obedience

"Elisha did not show his face to Naaman, but instead sent instructions: Wash yourself in the Jordan River seven times. The waters will heal you, and your skin will be back to normal. You will be cleansed." 2 King 5:10

Once you begin executing your vision, God's going to start downloading instructions during your meditation time, throughout the day, or even in your dreams. It's imperative to follow His instructions. It's going to take obedience and trust to follow His requests because most often, they won't make sense. If you find yourself asking, "Are you sure you want me to do or say that God," it's likely the direction you need to follow the most.

Once, a close friend was searching for her dream home. She sought God, boldly wrote and rewrote the vision daily, prayed, meditated, and even purchased a key chain inscribed, **My first home**. Once she embarked on house hunting, everything began falling into place...that is until God took her to a less than desired neighborhood to buy a fixer upper.

She asked God if He was certain that house was what He had for her. Her faith was so strong, she decided to forego her brand new five-bedroom home and purchased an old fixer upper on an unpleasant part of town. She had to move in with her mother while she waited for the renovations to start, and as much as she loved her mother, living with her parent wasn't what my friend envisioned as a middle-aged woman with three children.

Right before the renovations started, a gentleman stopped by asking if she'd be willing to sell her home, which made her wonder what God's plan truly was. She'd been obedient in following the vision, even sacrificing her dream home. Now before she could get started, she was supposed to sell. What she didn't know was that the home she bought was next to a lot that an investor recently purchased, and he needed her land to fit the houses in. She was able to sell her home for twice what she was willing to pay for her new construction.

God wants the best for us, not what we think is the best for ourselves. When He gives instruction, it's to protect, elevate, and give us more than we can imagine.

Take action:

Practice listening for God's instructions by asking Him for clear direction during your prayer time, then listen for the answer. Write down what He tells you to do, how you followed through with it, and what the outcome was. It may not be as life changing as buying a house; it could be as simple as taking a different route home, encouraging a stranger, or sending a kind note to a friend out of the blue.

_____

_____

_____

_____

Aim higher & Dream Bigger

"I am the vine; you are the branches. Whoever abides in Me and I in him, he it is that bears much fruit, for apart from Me you can do nothing." John 15:5

More than we can ask or think.
Be bold, believe, become.

I was listening to Sarah Jakes-Roberts when something she said struck me. Not that it was incredibly profound, but it awakened something in me. She said, "Be bold enough to ask God for something that's not even in your bloodline."

We sometimes place limitations on God or ask for things we think we're worthy of based on our own assumptions, lineage, and ability. But the word of God says that if you ask, you shall receive. It doesn't say if you've never been to jail, ask and you shall receive, or only if you come from a prestigious family, then you can ask. There's no precursor...it simply says ask.

The Word also says God will supply all our needs according to His riches, not ours. So, be bold and ask God for extraordinary favor, healing, blessings. If you have a desire to do something amazing like run for president, create a billion-dollar business, open a school, buy all the real estate in a section of the city, etc. – ASK. If no one in your family has ever had a successful marriage, international business, or good health, don't let that keep you from asking God to fulfill your desires.

It's important to get comfortable trusting God for that which we can't produce ourselves. It makes us dream bigger, reach higher, and accomplish more. Don't worry that no one in your family has ever done it, that you don't have all of the credentials, or your background is blemished. Be bold enough to ask God, confident enough to believe He'll open doors for you, and consistent enough to become what you desire.

As you execute on your vision, keep dreaming big, aiming higher and being bold enough to move forward towards everything God has in store for you.

I can't wait to see what you'll accomplish!

About the Author

Stacey Bawuuna is the owner of the Prepped Mom LLC, a lifestyle company providing change leadership, coaching and living-well expertise focused on empowering individuals to deliver value through purpose and thoughtful prioritization. Stacey's experience embodies her strong spiritual connection with God, with more than a decade of developing high performing teams, marrying strategy to execution and delivering solutions as a global leader for Fortune 100 and 500 companies.

Stacey's knack for bridging the gap between vision and execution was the inspiration for her book, as well as her podcast, **Morning Mugs with the Prepped Mom**, aimed at preparing to receive God's promises through prayer, prioritization and execution. In addition to corporate experience, *The Prepped Mom* is well known for preparing simple meals from everyday foods, repurposing items to create breathtaking decor, and hosting events on a budget, making each guest feel like family. Amongst the titles that Stacey has held, her most important are wife, mother, daughter, sister and friend.

CPSIA information can be obtained
at www.ICGtesting.com
Printed in the USA
LVHW011117210121
676968LV00007B/765

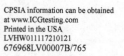

9 781736 411223